Yankees
2009
Phillies

Yankees
2000
Mets

Phillies
2008
Rays

Diamondbacks
2001
Yankees

WORLD SERIES SHOWDOWNS

Red Sox
2007
Rockies

Angels
2002
Giants

Richard J. Brenner

Cardinals
2006
Tigers

Marlins
2003
Yankees

White Sox
2005
Astros

Red Sox
2004
Cardinals

WORLD SERIES CHAMPIONS

EAST END PUBLISHING, LTD.
Miller Place, New York

This book is dedicated to Jackie Robinson for teaching me that talent devoid of dignity and courage is hollow and to President Barack Obama, whose uplifting vision of world peace, individual rights, universal opportunity, and environmental sanity, I admire and support. It is also dedicated to the children of the world. I wish that each of you get to live in a world like the one envisioned by Mr. Obama and that you do your part by striding toward that vision with courage and compassion, for yourself and for others. With great appreciation to Pete Seeger and Bob Dylan, who keep making music that rings out with passion and righteousness; to Pablo Picasso, for painting until the end and for giving us a vivid glimpse into what the end might look like, and to Johann Sebastian Bach, for his Cello Suites, and to Yo-Yo Ma, whose interpretation of those suites kept me company while I created this book.

My sincere thanks go to Ed Masessa, Janet Speakman, Roy Wandelmaier, and Alan Boyko, who gave me the opportunity to create this book. I also want to thank some of the people who assisted my efforts, including John Douglas, Alfred Mercado, Sarah Becker, Tamyka Muse, and Elliot Markham.

Book Designer: **Alfred Mercado**   Copy Editor: **John Douglas**

Photo Credits: The image of Derek Jeter on the cover and on P. 5, as well as the one of Mariano Rivera on P. 6 were photographed by **Anthony J. Causi** and supplied by Icon/SMI. Icon/SMI also supplied the images listed below, with the photographer's name in bold: P. 14 & 15, **Tom Hauck**; P. 16, **John Cordes**; P.21, **Jeff Zelevansky**; P. 34, **J.H. Gonzalez**/Detroit Free Press/Zuma Press; P. 41, Philadelphia DailyNews/Zuma Press. The World Series Trophy that appears throughout was photographed by **William A. Guerro**. The remaining photographs were supplied by Getty Images, as listed below: P. 8, **Brian Bahr**; P. 9, **Matthew Stockman**, P. 10, **Jed Jacobsohn**; P. 18 and P. 20, **Ezra Shaw**. P. 24, **Jed Jacobsohn**; P. 25, **Ron Vesely**; P. 26, **Ezra Shaw**. P. 29, **Jed Jacobsohn**; P. 30, **Rich Pilling**/Major League Baseball; P. 33, **Brad Mangin/MLB**; P. 37, **Elsa**; P. 38, **Jim McIsaac**; P. 42, **Doug Pensinger**; P. 44, **Jed Jacobsohn**; P. 46, N/A. P. 47, **Rich Pilling/MLB**.

ISBN: 0-943403-77-4 * 978-0-943403-77-9

Published by EAST END PUBLISHING, LTD.
18 Harbor Beach Road
Miller Place, NY 11764

Printed in the United States of America by Universal Printing Co.

Richard J. Brenner, America's best-selling sportswriter, has written more than 80 exciting sports titles. To order some of the available titles, send an email to: rjbrenner1@gmail.com.

*   *   *

Mr. Brenner is also available to speak at schools and other venues. For details, including fees, you may e-mail him directly at: rjbrenner1@gmail.com, or write to him c/o EEP, **18 Harbor Beach Road, Miller Place, NY 11764.**

AUTHOR'S MESSAGE: For many years, Native American groups have been appealing to sports teams not to use names and logos that many people find offensive. Out of respect for, and in support of those appeals, I have chosen not to use such names in this book.

This book was not authorized by Major League Baseball or by any of the players or teams mentioned in this book.

NEW YORK YANKEES 2000 NEW YORK METS

The 2000 World Series showdown between the New York Yankees and New York Mets was called the *Subway Series,* because fans could go from Yankee Stadium to Shea Stadium by using the New York City subway system. It was the first *Subway Series* since 1956, when the Yankees beat the Brooklyn Dodgers, a year before the *Bums* moved to Los Angeles.

The Mets had finished second in the National League East, a game behind Atlanta, but their 94-68 record was the best among the league's second-place finishers, making them the league's wild-card entry into the postseason. They faced the task of traveling across the country to meet the team with the majors' best record in 2000, the San Francisco Giants, in the Divisional series. But after they dropped the first game, the Mets reeled off three straight victories and they did it with style. They won the second game in 11 innings, but only after a heart-pounding save by veteran reliever John Franco, who fanned Barry Bonds, the game's most feared hitter, on a wicked 3–2 changeup. They won the third game in the 13th inning, when outfielder Benny Agbayani blasted a

ball into the third deck at Shea Stadium. In the finale, Bobby Jones hurled a one-hit shutout, getting Bonds for the last out.

The Mets' pennant chase took them to St. Louis to play the Central division champion Cardinals, who had swept their Division series against Atlanta. It marked the first time since 1992 that Atlanta hadn't reached the League Championship Series. The Mets continued their hot streak by sweeping two games at Busch Stadium and, when the series shifted to Shea, the Mets took two of the three and advanced to the World Series on the strength of another pitching gem; this time by their ace Mike Hampton, who dealt a three-hit shutout against the Cards.

Although the Yankees had won three of the previous four World Series, the 2000 version of the team seemed more ordinary than special. While they had won the Eastern Division title, their 87 wins looked commonplace compared to the 98 totaled by the 1999 team, and the 114 posted by the 1998 squad, the most wins by a Major League team since the Chicago Cubs had won 116 in 1906.

The Yankees opened the defense of the World Series titles they had won the previous two seasons by barely winning a challenging five-game series against the West division champion Oakland Athletics.

"That was so hard," said center fielder Bernie Williams, stretching out the words to emphasize the effort that had been spent and the relief that he felt at being able to move on to the LCS. "But it's not going to get any easier."

The Yankees split the first two home games against the wild-card-winning Mariners, who had ousted the Chicago White Sox. The series then moved to Safeco Field, where the Yankees took two-of-three, including a one-hit *time capsule* performance by Roger Clemens, who set an ALCS record with 15 strikeouts. The sixth game, back at the Stadium, turned into a slugfest, which the Yankees won, 9-7, to earn their 37th pennant and set up the inter-borough face-off.

"The city has been looking for this match-up for a long time," declared Yankees' outfielder David Justice, who hit a three-run homer in game 6 and was named the LCS MVP. "New York is going to be on fire for the next week-and-a-half."

Justice ignited the first flame in Game 1 by breaking a scoreless tie with a two-run double in the bottom of the sixth inning at Yankee Stadium. The Mets, who were stymied by their own inept base-running earlier in the game and by an extraordinary defensive play by Yankees' shortstop Derek Jeter, managed to scratch out three runs in the top of the seventh and they took that slim one-run lead into the bottom of the ninth. But the Mets' closer, Armando Benitez, allowed the Yankees to tie the score on a sacrifice fly that sent the game into extra innings. The Yankees wasted a scoring opportunity in the tenth when two of their most reliable hitters, Tino Martinez and Paul O'Neill, left a runner stranded at third base with less than two outs. Two innings later, however, reserve second baseman Jose Vizcaino finally ended the longest game in World Series history with his fourth hit of the game, a two-out single that scored Martinez with the winning run.

The loss was a bitter pill for the Mets, who realized that they had thrown away Game 1 with their own sloppy play on the base paths. And Game 2 didn't do anything for their spirits, either, as the Yankees exploded for six first-inning runs, while Clemens put up goose eggs for eight innings. Even after the Mets stormed back with five ninth-inning runs off the Yankees bullpen, Mariano Rivera, the shutdown artist, slammed the door and preserved a 6-5 win for the Bronx Bombers.

The Series shifted to Shea and the outlook seemed dim for the Mets, because the Yankees' starter was Orlando Hernandez and *El Duque*, the Cuban-born right-hander, had an 8-0 mark

The Mets' win in Game 3 snapped the Yankees' 14-game World Series winning streak that had started in 1996.

The Yankees were the first team to three-peat as World Series champions since the 1972-74 Oakland Athletics.

DEREK JETER
2000 WORLD SERIES MVP

MARIANO RIVERA

in postseason play. But the Mets put an end to his perfect record, as Agbayani drove in the go-ahead run in a two-run, eighth-inning rally that provided the margin of victory in a 4-2 win.

As if to blunt any emerging hopes, Jeter hit the first pitch of Game 4 over the fence. After the Yanks tacked on another run in the second inning, Jeter struck again in the third, when he tripled and came in to score the Yankees' third run. Although the Mets clawed back to within a run when Mike Piazza launched a two-run home run in the bottom of the third, that was as close as they would get.

"This has been a gut-wrenching Series," noted Paul O'Neill. "Each of our three wins have been by one run and, when we walk off the field, we know we've been in a battle."

Game 5 also turned into a gut-churner, as the teams went into the ninth inning tied, 2-2, the Mets having scrounged out two unearned runs off of Andy Pettitte to answer solo homers by Williams and Jeter, who was named the Series MVP. Al Leiter, the Mets' starter, struck out the first two batters in the ninth, but then gave up a walk and a single before second baseman Luis Sojo squirted a single through the infield to give the Yankees a 4-2 lead. The Mets' last gasp hopes were extinguished by Rivera, allowing the Yankees to exhale and celebrate their third straight World Series win and the 26th, overall, in franchise history.

"I know that a lot of people criticized this team," said Yankees' manager Joe Torre. "But we can put our dedication and resolve against any team that's ever played the game of baseball."

The 2001 World Series featured one team, the New York Yankees, that was going for its fourth straight title under manager Joe Torre and had the mystique of 26 Series pennants flying at the world-renowned Yankee Stadium; while the other team, the Arizona Diamondbacks, a fourth-year expansion franchise, was playing in its first World Series. But neither the D-backs' players nor their manager, Bob Brenly, seemed cowed by their opponents' past glories.

"We don't buy into all the hype in the media," said Brenly, who had piloted the D-backs to the National League West title. "We're not playing against Babe Ruth or Lou Gehrig; it's all about the present."

The Yankees didn't have anyone who approached the achievements of *The Sultan of Swat* or *the Iron Horse*. Only shortstop Derek Jeter ranked among the American League leaders in batting average and first baseman Tino Martinez was the only member of the cast to finish in the top ten in home runs and RBI. Center fielder Bernie Williams and catcher Jorge Posada were, as usual, reliable run-producers and rookie second baseman

Alfonso Soriano had added some pop and speed. They were strong at the top of their starting pitching staff, where Cy Young Award-winner Roger Clemens, with a 20-3 mark, led the way. Mike Mussina and Andy Pettitte, who totaled 32 wins between them, followed him in the rotation. The bullpen was another area of strength, highlighted by the unmatchable Mariano Rivera, who'd led the league with 50 saves. They were, in short, a solid, savvy, mostly veteran team, who had won the East division title by a comfortable margin, and they welcomed the Oakland Athletics into the Stadium for the start of the Division series.

The A's, who had won seven more games during the season than their hosts, proved to be undesirable guests, however, by taking the first two games. The series moved to Oakland, with the Yankees needing a win to survive; and they did, but just barely, as Mussina and Rivera combined to shut out Oakland, while Posada provided the only run in the game with a solo homer. Jeter made the defensive play of the series in the seventh when he snared an errant relay throw near the first base line and back-

LUIS GONZALEZ

handed a toss to Posada, cutting down the potential tying run at the plate. The Yankees ended their trip to the brink by taking the next two games and moving into the League Championship Series against the Seattle Mariners. Then they cold-cocked the Mariners, who had tied a Major League record by winning 116 games, by taking four of five, with Rivera notching saves in three of the games.

Arizona didn't have any individual stars on offense, except for left fielder Luis Gonzalez, who had a career year, with 57 home runs and 142 RBI. The two other outfielders, Reggie Sanders and Steve Finley, were consistent run producers, as were the corner infielders, Mark Grace and Matt Williams, while Tony Womack, Jay Bell, and Craig Counsell were their mainstays in the middle infield.

What set Arizona apart, however, were its top two starters, 21-game-winner Randy Johnson, the lanky southpaw, who won his third straight Cy Young Award; and Curt Schilling, who tied for the league lead with 22 wins. There was a steep drop-off in the rotation after those twin jewels, however, and Byung-Hyun Kim, the team's closer, was young and relatively inexperienced.

Schilling started the team off on the right foot in the Division series with a tone-setting, three-hit shutout against St. Louis, earning the win when Steve Finley poked a home run against the Cardinals' ace, Matt Morris. St. Louis did not go quietly, however, and it took late-inning rallies in the fourth and fifth games and another pitching gem by Schilling to subdue the Cardinals. In the finale, Schilling

RANDY JOHNSON
2003 WORLD SERIES CO-MVP

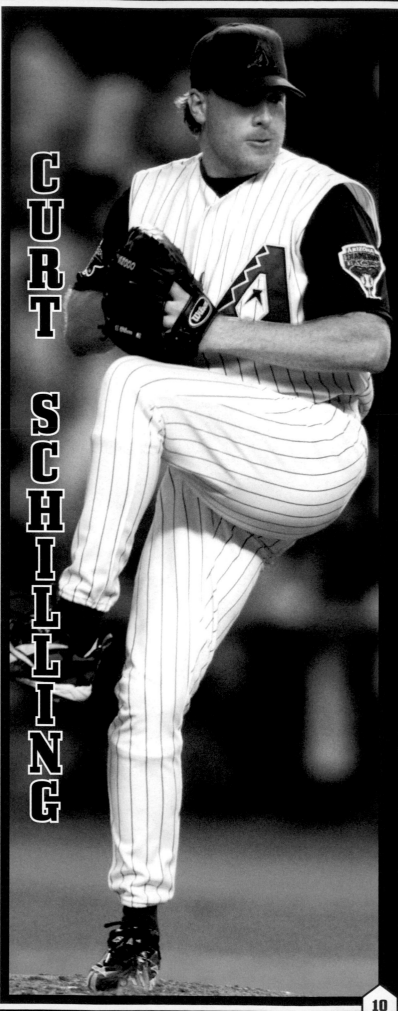

CURT SCHILLING

out-dueled Morris again, 2-1, but got the win only when Womack stroked an RBI single in the bottom of the ninth.

Johnson set the keynote in the opener of the LCS, when he whitewashed Atlanta, while Greg Counsell, who was named the series' MVP, scored the only two runs in the game. After a blowout loss in the second game, the D-backs turned to Schilling to get them back on track and he threw all the right switches, pitching them to a 5-1 win. Arizona's offense took charge in an 11-4 wipeout in the following game and then Johnson, with two innings of relief help from Kim, applied the coup de grace in a 3-2 win that sent them on to the World Series.

The D-backs, playing in front of their hometown fans in Bank One Ballpark, out-classed the Yankees in Game 1, chasing Mussina and beating the visitors, 9-1. Brenly pulled Schilling after the seventh inning, hoping to keep the big right-hander ready to go again on three days' rest.

"I'm not *possibly* available," declared Schilling. "I'm available. This is the World Series, and if he needs me in Game 4, I'll be ready."

Johnson stepped into the spotlight next, holding the Yankees scoreless, while Matt Williams delivered a three-run dinger in the D-backs' 4-0 win. It was the first complete game shutout in a World Series since Schilling had slammed the door on the Toronto Blue Jays while pitching for the Philadelphia Phillies in 1993.

"Randy was sensational," acknowledged Joe Torre. "Now we need to break the fall and, fortunately, we have Roger going for us in the next game."

Clemens gave Torre everything he had hoped for by going seven strong innings at the Stadium before handing the ball over to Rivera, who pitched the final two stanzas of the Yankees' 2-1 win. Posada backed Clemens with a second-inning homer and third baseman Scott Brosius' two-out single in the sixth brought home Bernie Williams with the game-winner.

Schilling, as promised, took the ball in Game 4 and he delivered on cue, holding the Yankees to three hits over seven innings before turning the ball and a 3-1 lead over to Byung-Hyun Kim. The young closer looked unhittable in the eighth, striking out the side and, even after right fielder Paul O'Neill stroked a one-out single in the bottom of the ninth, Kim fanned Bernie Williams for the second out. Then Tino Martinez, who had been hitless in the Series, stunned the D-backs by stroking a game-tying home run over the right field wall. One inning later, Jeter, who was 1-15, completed the dramatic comeback by drilling another Kim delivery for a walk-off homer.

"The beauty of the postseason is that it doesn't matter what you've done up to a certain point," said Jeter. "Every time you're at the plate or in the field, you have the opportunity to do something special. You never know when your opportunity will come."

The following night, Kim was again trying to protect a two-run lead with two outs in the ninth inning but lightning struck for a second time when third baseman Scott Brosius tagged him

Randy Johnson and Curt Schilling, who combined for a 4-0 record, shared the 2001 World Series MVP Award.

This was the first time that a team who had trailed entering the final inning won the World Series.

for another game-tying home run. Three innings later, Alfonso Soriano ended the marathon with an RBI hit, putting the Yankees up three-games-to-two.

The gut-churning tension of the previous two games turned into comic relief, as the D-backs, with Johnson on the mound, delighted their hometown fans with a 15-2 win, turning the Series into a one-game showdown and a fantasy league pitching match-up.

"It's the seventh game of the World Series and we're going against Roger Clemens and the Yankees," said Schilling. "*How cool is that?*"

Game 7, turned into a white-knuckled affair, as Clemens and Schilling kept the scoreboard empty of runs until the D-backs broke through for one in the sixth. The Yankees, who had been held to just one hit by Schilling, tied the score in the seventh and then took a 2-1 lead on Soriano's homer in the eighth. Then Rivera, who was asked to get six outs, struck out the side in the bottom of the eighth to preserve the lead. In the bottom of the ninth, however, the supreme closer faulted and, after Womack had delivered a game-tying double, Luis Gonzalez hit a pop fly, World Series-winning single, just over the head of Jeter, who had been drawn in for a play at the plate.

"All through the Series we were hearing about the aura and mystique of the Yankees; well our aura and mystique are Curt and Randy," declared Mark Grace, "and they were good enough for us."

Although it wasn't nearly as local as a Subway Series, the 2002 Fall Classic was still something of a regional affair, with the San Francisco Giants squaring off against an interstate rival, the Anaheim Angels.

The Giants, who had finished the regular season behind the defending champion Diamondbacks in the NL West, were trying to capture their first title since the franchise moved from Manhattan to San Francisco in 1958. The Angels, meanwhile, had been the runner-up in the AL West, and they were trying to win the first Series in their 42-year history.

The cornerstones of the Giants' team were left fielder Barry Bonds, who led the majors with a .370 average while winning the fifth of his seven MVP awards, and their hard-hitting second basemen Jeff Kent, who had won the award two years earlier. That dynamic duo had combined for a total of 86 home runs and 218 RBI, and additional punch was provided by right fielder Reggie Sanders, who smacked 23 big flies, and third baseman David Bell, who poked 20 dingers. Although the pitching staff didn't feature a certifiable ace at the top

of the rotation, they did have five starters who each won between 12 and 14 games, and an All-Star closer, Robb Nen.

San Francisco took its first playoff step by slipping past Atlanta, who pushed them to the limit in the best-of-five Division series. The Giants, in fact, had their backs to the wall after dropping two of the first three games, but they staved off elimination at home with an 8-3 win at Pacific Bell Park, as shortstop Rich Aurilia drilled a two-run homer and collected four RBI. The teams then traveled across the country to Turner Field for the decisive fifth game, which the Giants won 3-1. Bonds, rising to the occasion, tallied the winning run with his third round-tripper of the series, while the pitching of Russ Ortiz and a quartet of relievers held Atlanta's bats at bay.

The Giants went on to take four of five from the St. Louis Cardinals in the LCS, including a come-from-behind 2-1 victory in the finale, in which Bonds hit a game-tying sacrifice fly in the eighth inning, and center fielder Kenny Lofton drove in the pennant-clinching run with a ninth inning single.

The Angels top players included first baseman Troy Glaus and left fielder Garret Anderson, who had both finished among the league leaders in home runs and RBI. They also received strong production from right fielder Tim Salmon, third baseman Scott Spiezio, second baseman Adam Kennedy, and their top of the order table-setters, center fielder Darren Erstad, and the pint-sized shortstop David Eckstein. The pitching staff featured a trio of starters who had won 14 or more games, topped by 18-game winner Jarrod Washburn, and closer Troy Percival.

Their postseason got off to a shaky start when they went on the road and dropped the opening game of the Division series to the Yankees, despite a pair of home runs by Glaus. And they looked as though they might be headed for a quick exit when they fell behind late in the second game, but Anderson and Glaus hit back-to-back homers in the eighth inning and the Angels rallied to win 8-6. The scene shifted to Anaheim's Edison International Field for the next game, and the Angels offered their fans another high wire act before they staged their second consecutive three-run, eighth inning rally and held on for a 9-6 win. The winning pitcher was the 20-year-old rookie reliever Francisco Rodriguez, A.K.A. K-Rod, who had pitched a total of only 5.1 regular-season innings in the majors.

The Angels took most of the excitement out of the fourth game by scoring eight runs in the fifth inning, as they knocked off the Yankees, who had won four consecutive pennants. The Angels then faced off against the Minnesota Twins in the ALCS and, after stubbing their toes with a 2-1 loss in the first game, the Angels reeled off four straight wins, including the finale, when Adam Kennedy led an 18-hit parade with three dingers and five RBI. As the players and coaching staff celebrated the first pennant in franchise history on the field, their frenzied red-clad fans stood and cheered, and banged their ThunderStix in joyful appreciation.

But neither the noisemakers nor the scoreboard's electronic cartoon Rally Monkey came to the Angels' rescue in Game 1 of the World Series, as Washburn served up second inning home runs to Bonds and Reggie Sanders and a two-run shot to J.T. Snow in the sixth that turned out to be the winning blow in a 4-3 Giants' win.

"Obviously, you want to win every game," said Glaus, who had done his part by slamming a pair of solo homers. "But if we can take anything out of the loss, it's that we've been here before, we have a job to do and we know how to do it."

The Angels' offense clearly demonstrated that they were up to the task by tagging Giants' starter Russ Ortiz for five first inning runs in Game 2. But their starting pitcher, Kevin Appier, and two relievers gave back all of that and more, as the Giants cracked

Troy Glaus, who batted .385 with three homers and eight RBI, was named the Series MVP.

John Lackey became the first rookie in 93 years to win a Game 7 in the World Series.

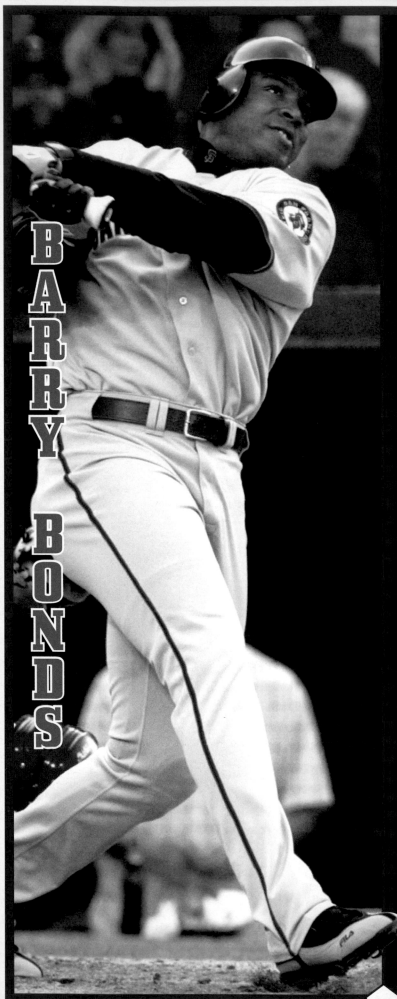

BARRY BONDS

three home runs on their way to a 9-7 lead in the top of the fifth. Angels' manager Mike Scioscia finally found a way to stop the assault at the start of the sixth stanza, when he gave the ball to K-Rod. While the rookie provided three innings of perfection on the mound, the Angels scored single runs in the fifth and sixth innings and then retook the lead, 11-9, on a two-run eighth-inning dinger by Tim Salmon, his second big blast of the game. Percival closed out the contest, despite yielding a long home run to Bonds; while Rodriguez earned the victory, the Angels first-ever World Series win.

"I can't believe this is happening," said K-Rod, after learning that he had tied Randy Johnson's record of five wins in a single postseason. "If I'm dreaming, I don't want to wake up."

The scene shifted north to San Francisco, but the Angels' bats stayed red-hot for another game, and they roasted the Giants, 10-4, despite another home run by Bonds, his record-breaking seventh big fly of the postseason. The Giants, however, came back to tie the Series with a 4-3 win, and then clobbered the Angels, 16-4, to take a 3-games-to-2 lead.

The action returned to Anaheim for Game 6, and the Giants went for the jugular, as yet another Bonds home run helped stake them to a 5-0 seventh inning lead. With the Angels facing elimination and down to their last eight outs, Glaus singled to left, Fullmer singled to right, and Spiezio ripped a three-run homer that brought the hometown fans out of their seats.

"It seemed like it took half an hour to

TROY GLAUS
2002 WORLD SERIES MVP

FRANCISCO RODRIGUEZ

get over the fence," said Spiezio, who tied a postseason record with his 19th RBI. "It was the longest few seconds of my life."

Erstad cut the deficit to a single run with a leadoff homer in the bottom of the eighth, and three batters later Glaus lined a two-run double to left center off Giants' closer Robb Nen that vaulted the Angels to a Series-saving 6-5 victory.

After all the drama of the previous game, Game 7 seemed almost low key as the Angels rode a three-run third-inning double by Garret Anderson, five quality innings by John Lackey and four shutout innings by a trio of relievers to a 4-1 win and their first World Series championship.

"It took every single one to win this," said Percival, who closed out the game with his third save of the Series. "We had a goal at the beginning of the year, and we stayed true to it all the way through to the end."

Mike Scioscia, who was named the AL Manager of the Year for turning around a team that had finished 41 games out of first place the previous year, echoed his closer's words.

"This championship was about 25 guys on the field giving everything they had," said Scioscia, who had, by coincidence, been a teammate of Giants' manager Dusty Baker on the 1981 Los Angeles Dodgers' World Series-winning team. "Winning the World Series is about the players on the field. I've never been around a group of guys who have worked so hard to reach a goal."

On paper, the 2003 showdown between the Florida Marlins and the New York Yankees seemed as unbalanced as the battle between David and Goliath. The Yankees had won 101 games—10 more than the Marlins— and they had a line-up loaded with veteran stars, who had been tested in previous title runs, while the Marlins were heavily reliant on young players who didn't have any experience playing in pressure-packed postseason games.

The Yankees' title run got off to a quick start when they took three-of-four from the Minnesota Twins in the Division series. But the Yanks had to fight for their baseball lives in the LCS against the Boston Red Sox, before taking down the Boys from Beantown on an 11th inning, game-seven home run off the bat of third baseman Aaron Boone.

The wild-card-winning Marlins featured the speedy centerfielder and leadoff hitter, Juan Pierre, who led the majors with 65 stolen bases, while posting a .305 average, nine points behind second baseman Luis Castillo. The Fish also received solid production from shortstop Alex Gonzalez, right-fielder Juan Encarnacion, first baseman Derrek Lee and third baseman Mike Lowell, the team leader in homers and RBI.

Their pitching staff was built on the arms of its young starters, including Brad Penny, the emerging Josh Beckett, and the electrifying Dontrelle Willis, the NL Rookie of the Year. The Fish also fortified their bullpen with a midseason trade for closer Ugueth Urbina, but their biggest snare was free-agent catcher Ivan Rodriguez, who had been an automatic All-Star in his 11 seasons with the Texas Rangers. I-Rod, with a catapult for an arm, owned 10 Gold Gloves, six Silver Slugger awards, and the 1999 AL MVP trophy.

The Marlins started their postseason in San Francisco, where they split a pair of games with the Giants, the NL West division champions. After being shut out in the first game, the Marlins came back to out-slug the Giants, 9-6, in the second one. When the series moved east to Pro Player Stadium, I-Rod got the Marlins off to a quick start by jacking a two-run homer in the bottom of the first and his two-run single in the 11th pulled out a 4-3 win for the Fish. The Marlins closed out the

IVAN RODRGUEZ

Giants with another nail-biting victory, 7-6, protecting their lead on a game-ending strike from left fielder Jeff Conine to I-Rod, who slapped a tag on J.T. Snow and held onto the ball, despite being bowled over by the Giants' first baseman.

"We're a good team," said I-Rod. "Whoever plays against us has to play hard until the last out, because we're going to keep coming at them."

The Marlins traveled to Wrigley Field for the LCS, where they took on the Chicago Cubs, the Central division champions and upset winners over Atlanta in the Division series. The Marlins continued their string of dramatic wins when Mike Lowell drilled an 11th inning pinch-hit homer over the ivy-covered wall in left field to give them a 9-8 win over the Cubs in the opening game. But the streak came to a screeching halt, as the Marlins lost the next three games, including a pair at Pro Player Stadium. With no margin for error, the Fish stepped back from the brink on a brilliant performance by Josh Beckett, who stymied the Cubs with a two-hit shutout, and home runs by Lowell, Conine, and I-Rod. As the series switched back to Wrigley, the Fish were still faced with a win-or-go-home scenario, and it looked like the latter when the Cubs' ace, Mark Prior, took a 3-0 lead into the eighth inning of the sixth game. But a fan-interference play on a foul fly opened the floodgates for Florida and, Pierre, given a second chance to swing the stick, laced a double to start an eight-run, game-winning outburst. Pierre also jump-started the offense in game seven with a leadoff triple and eventually came in to score on a three-run jack by Miguel Cabrera. Although the Cubs rallied to take a 5-3 lead, the Marlins bounced right back and took the decisive game, 9-6.

Pierre also had his fingerprints all over Game 1 of the World Series, coming around to score the first run after opening the contest with a bunt single. Then, after Jeter had tied the game with an RBI single in the third, Pierre lined a fifth-inning single that knocked in two runs and provided the margin of victory in a 3-2 win at Yankee stadium.

Although the Yankees' staff snapped I-Rod's postseason hitting streak at 11 games, he did knock in the Marlin's first run with a sacrifice fly and he also short-circuited the Yankees' third-inning rally by picking off Nick Johnson at third base.

"When you play aggressive defense, good things are going to happen," said Rodriguez, the NLCS MVP. "If they take big leads, I'm going to throw. I'm not afraid to throw to bases."

For Game 2, Joe Torre placed the ball in the large left hand of Andy Pettitte, just as he had done in the second game of the series against the Red Sox and the Twins, and in so many other key-game assignments since Mr. Dependable had joined the staff in 1995. And, as usual, Pettitte delivered a masterly performance, holding the Marlins to six hits and one unearned run in 8.2 innings.

"He's been doing this all along," said Jeter. "When we need him to step up, he does."

The Yankees scored all the runs they would need on a three-run, first inning big fly by outfielder Hideki Matsui, who became the first Japanese player to hit a home run in a World Series and only the second one ever to play in one.

The scene shifted to Miami for Game 3 but the score remained the same, 6-1, as Mike Mussina, who yielded one run in seven innings, and Mariano Rivera all but iced the Marlins' bats. Beckett, who pitched 7.1 innings, was almost as effective for Florida, but the Yankees scratched out the go-ahead run on an RBI by Matsui off of Dontrelle Willis in the eighth and exploded for four runs in the ninth, three of them coming on a Bernie Williams home run.

The Marlins' bats finally thawed out in the first inning of Game 4 when their rookie slugger, Miguel Cabrera, cracked a two-run homer off of Roger Clemens, their first home run of the Series. But, after Derrek Lee added an RBI single later in the frame, the Marlins' hitters went back into the deep freeze. It didn't seem to matter at the time because Carl Pavano was limiting the Yankees to only one run in his eight innings of work. But Urbina couldn't close the deal, allowing the Yankees to tie the game on a two-out, two-run triple by Rubén Sierra. The

Josh Beckett's 47 strikeouts in 2003 tied the single post-season record set by Randy Johnson in 2001.

While the Marlins have never won a divisional title, they do own two World Series titles, 1997 and 2003.

BRAD PENNY

tension inside Pro Player swelled dramatically as Marlins' reliever Braden Looper doused a bases-loaded Yankees' threat in the top of the 11th inning, but then it burst into a moment of exquisite relief when Alex Gonzalez stroked a walk-off homer off of Jeff Weaver in the bottom of the inning that tied the Series at 2-2.

"We needed a big win," Derrek Lee noted. "Going down 3-1 in this series would have made it really tough to come back."

The Marlins also struck quickly in Game 5, building a 6-2 lead behind seven solid innings by starter Brad Penny, and then holding on for a 6-4 win when Bernie Williams' bid for a game-tying homer in the ninth was caught a few feet in front of the right field wall.

The Series returned to Yankee Stadium for Game 6 and 23-year-old Josh Beckett made sure that there wouldn't be a need for a Game 7 by pitching a five-hit shutout, leading the Marlins to a 2-0 win and the title.

"We wanted to play the Yankees because they have 26 championships," said Beckett, who was named the Series MVP. "And if you're going to beat somebody, why not beat the best?"

Although most baseball fans were surprised by the Marlins' win over the Goliath-like Yankees, Jeff Conine didn't think that their triumph was even an upset.

"We were the hottest team in baseball at the end of the season and through the playoffs," he noted. "Even though most people didn't give us a chance, we knew we could win and we proved it."

JOSH BECKETT
2003 WORLD SERIES MVP

The 2004 World Series featured the St. Louis Cardinals and the Boston Red Sox, franchises with long, rich traditions. The Redbirds' history included Hall of Famers' Rogers Hornsby, whose career average of .359 is the highest-ever in the National League; Stan Musial, who captured seven batting titles, and Bob Gibson, a two-time World Series MVP. Their back-story also included a league-record nine World Series championships, the latest of which had been captured in 1982. Boston also had an impressive list of Hall of Famers, including Cy Young, the winningest pitcher of all time; Ted Williams, the last player to hit .400, and Carl Yastrzemski, the last one to win batting's Triple Crown. The Red Sox' family tree showed five World Series titles, including the first one, in 1903, when CY Young won two of the games, and four more between 1912 and 1918. But that was the last time they'd won a World Series and a legend developed that their lack of titles was the direct result of Boston's sale of Babe Ruth to the New York Yankees in December 1919. The so-called *Curse of the Bambino* loomed over four futile trips to the Series since that deal, the most recent of which

was an agonizing seven-game loss to the New York Mets in 1986.

The Cardinals had romped to the Central division title and led the majors with 105 wins. They had hammered 214 home runs, while leading the league in most batting categories, and their pitching staff posted the second-lowest ERA in the NL. The big chips in the middle of the Cards' order were first baseman Albert Pujols, the best right-handed hitter in the league, third baseman Scott Rolen and center fielder Jim Edmonds, who were known collectively as the *MV3*. Larry Walker, a three-time batting champion, was added to the potent lineup in a mid-season trade and shortstop Edgar Renteria and second baseman Tony Womack were accomplished table-setters. Although the pitching staff wasn't littered with Cy Young Award candidates in 2004, four of their starters had won 15 or more games and closer Jason Isringhausen had rung up 47 saves.

The Cardinals made quick work of the West division-champion Los Angeles Dodgers in the Division series, taking three of the four games. But there was nothing quick or easy about their LCS clash against the wild-card-winning

Houston Astros, which developed into one of the most exciting encounters in postseason history. On one level, the series played out as a riveting personal duel between Albert Pujols and the Astros' center fielder Carlos Beltran, who had demolished Atlanta's top-ranked pitching staff in their divisional series by hitting four dingers and driving in nine runs, five of them in the fifth-game finale. The switch-hitting Beltran continued his astonishing production against the Cardinals by belting four more big flies, which tied the postseason record of eight that had been set in 2002 by Barry Bonds. In the end, however, Pujols and the Cardinals prevailed in a seven-game barnburner, with *Big Albert* clouting a game-winning big fly in the opener and scoring the winning runs in the final two must-win contests.

"Going to the Word Series is what you dream about when you're a little boy," said a joyous Pujols, who hit .500, with four homers and nine RBI and was named the MVP of the LCS. "It doesn't get any better than this."

The Red Sox had finished three games behind the Yankees in the American League East but their 98 wins were six games better than the Central and Western division champions, the Minnesota Twins and the Anaheim Angels. Boston's best-in-the-league offense featured left-fielder Manny Ramirez and designated-hitter David Ortiz, who had tallied 269 RBI between them while finishing one-two in the AL in home runs. Center fielder and leadoff

hitter Johnny Damon finished third on the team in home runs and RBI, while posting a .304 average. Other key contributors on offense included catcher Jason Varitek, first baseman Kevin Millar, second baseman Mark Bellhorn, third basemen Bill Mueller, and shortstop Orlando Cabrera. Boston's deep starting pitching staff was headed by Curt Schilling, who had signed as a free agent, Pedro Martinez, a three-time Cy Young Award-winner, and Derek Lowe, while closer Keith Foulke rounded out a formidable bullpen.

The Red Sox swept three straight from the Angels in the Division series, setting up an LCS clash against their arch-nemesis, the New York Yankees, who had taken down the Twins in the other Division series. The BoSox had been sucking Yankee fumes for decades, suffering through a long string of second-place finishes and crushing defeats in critical games against their division rivals, including the seventh game of the 2003 LCS and their painful loss in the 1978 pennant-playoff.

The 2004 season had run true to form, with the Yankees topping Boston in the divisional race, and, after the BoSox had dropped the first three games of the LCS, it didn't appear as if the second-fiddle role was about to change. The embarrassing 19-8 drubbing they suffered in front of their hometown fans at Fenway Park in game three made it seem as though they were an inconsequential stepping stone to another Yankees' triumph. Boston was not only

The Red Sox became the fourth team to never trail during a World Series and the first since 1989.

The Red Sox became the first team to win eight consecutive games in a single postseason.

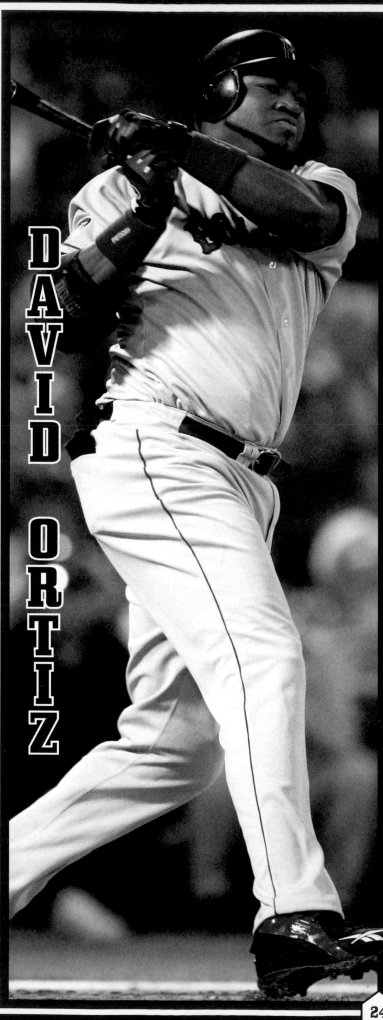

DAVID ORTIZ

playing against the Yankees at this point but challenging history, as well, because no major league baseball team had ever come back from a 3-0 postseason deficit; and after that third-game rout, the Red Sox didn't appear capable of rebounding and reversing that trend line. But, just as they were standing at the edge of the cliff in the ninth inning of game four and facing the game's premiere closer, Mariano Rivera, they rallied to tie the game when pinch-runner Dave Roberts swiped second base and came in to score on a single by Bill Mueller. Three innings later, David Ortiz, affectionately known as *Big Papi* by the Fenway faithful, kept their hopes alive with a walk-off big fly over the right field wall. The BoSox pulled off another late-game rally in game five and then Ortiz, who had homered in the eighth, delivered a two-out, game-winning single in the 14th inning. The Red Sox roared into Yankee Stadium and tied the series with a 4-2 win, as Curt Schilling and the bullpen held the Yankees' hitters in check and Mark Bellhorn blasted a three-run home run. Ortiz, who was named the LCS MVP, got the ball rolling in the first inning of game seven with a two-run dinger and Johnny Damon kept it going with a grand slam in the fourth, as the Red Sox battered the Yankees, 10-3, and completed the biggest comeback in postseason history.

After their epic win over the Yankees, it would have been understandable if the Red Sox were emotionally flat for Game 1 of the World Series. Instead of sagging, however, the BoSox soared, out-slugging the Cardinals, 10-8, in front of a delighted, full-house crowd at

MANNY RAMIREZ
2004 WORLD SERIES MVP

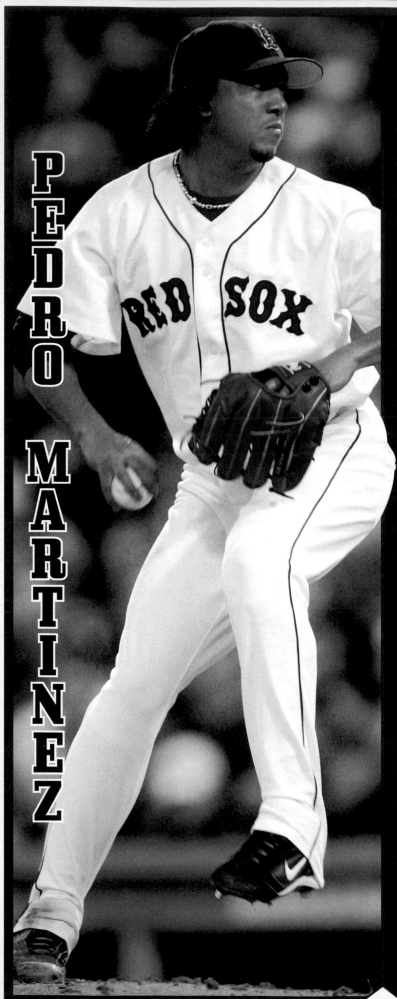

PEDRO MARTINEZ

Fenway. Ortiz ignited the fireworks with a three-run big fly in his first at-bat in a World Series and Bellhorn belted the two-run game-winning homer in the eighth.

"Let me tell you, we didn't play that well," said Ortiz, speaking about the team's four errors. "I hope we come back and play better tomorrow."

Boston kept its momentum moving forward with a 6-2 win in Game 2, as Curt Schilling, with three innings of help from the bullpen, led the way from the mound. Jason Varitek got the scoring started with a two-run triple in the first, while Mueller and Bellhorn hit back-to-back RBI doubles in the fourth and Orlando Cabrera closed out their scoring with a two-run single in the sixth.

The Series shifted to Busch Stadium but the home field didn't prove advantageous for the Cardinals. Pedro Martinez shut them out for seven innings and Manny Ramirez collected a pair of RBI, including a first-inning home run, as the Boston express kept rolling with a 4-1 win. If the Cardinals had any thoughts of duplicating the breathless four-game surge that the BoSox had initiated against the Yankees, they were quickly dispelled. Damon gave the Red Sox all the runs they would need in Game 4 when he whacked a leadoff homer, because Derek Lowe and the bullpen shut out the Cardinals, as Boston swept away the Cardinals and *The Curse* by winning its first World Series in 86 years.

"This is what we've all been waiting for," said general manager Theo Epstein. "Now, we can die happy."

The 2005 World Series pitted the Chicago White Sox, a franchise that hadn't won a Series in 87 years, against the Houston Astros, a club that was making its first-ever appearance in the Fall Classic after 43 years of futility. The Sox' general manager, Ken Williams, was so distraught by the drought, which was the second-longest behind the Chicago Cubs' streak of 96 years, that he didn't even attend the 2004 Series, let alone join in the 86-year, famine-ending celebration of Red Sox Nation.

"I'm not going out there to see other teams have the fun I want to have with our fans and organization," said Williams. "I couldn't even pass by the television without getting upset."

The White Sox gave themselves a chance to make it to the Series by winning the American League Central division title with a league-high 99 wins. The *Big Bopper* in Chicago's offense was first baseman Paul Konerko, who hit 40 homers and drove in 100 runs, and his supporting cast included third baseman Joe Crede, right fielder Jermaine Dye, and left fielder and leadoff hitter Scott Podsednik, who swiped 59 bases. The team's greatest strength, however, was its starting pitching staff, which included Mark Buehrle, Freddy Garcia, Jon Garland, and Jose Contreras, but it also received a big boost from the fire-balling rookie-closer Bobby Jenks.

Chicago boosted its postseason prospects by sweeping the defending champion Boston Red Sox in the Division series, before moving on to the League Championship Series against the Los Angeles Angels of Anaheim, the West division titleists (who seemed to be in a never-ending pursuit to find the franchise's final name). Although Chicago was tripped up at home in the series opener, they rode four-straight quality starts and some timely hitting by Crede and Konerko, the LCS MVP, into the World Series for the first time in 46 years.

The Astros entered the postseason as the National League's wild-card team and, like Chicago, they relied heavily on their pitching staff, which featured starters Roy Oswalt and a pair of former and future New York Yankee stalwarts, Andy Pettitte and Roger Clemens; while closer Brad Lidge contributed 42 saves. The big bats in the lineup belonged to their corner infielders, Lance Berkman and Morton

Ensberg, who led the team in home runs and RBI, and outfielder Jason Lane, while center fielder Willy Taveras, the league's Rookie of the Year, provided speed at the top of the order. The Astros began their playoff mission by taking three-of-four from Atlanta, including an amazing comeback win in the finale, when Berkman hit a grand slam in the eighth and catcher Brad Asmus tied the score with a two-out dinger in the ninth. But they didn't close the deal until nine innings later, when Chris Burke ended the longest game in postseason history with a walk-off big fly in the 18th inning.

In the LCS, the stoked Astros then met the Central division-champion St. Louis Cardinals, a team that featured the league's MVP, Albert Pujols, and its Cy Young Award-winner, Chris Carpenter. St. Louis not only had star power over the Astros, they had also led the majors in victories and finished 11 lengths in front of Houston, their rivals in the division. The Cardinals, moreover, had beaten the Astros in the 2004 LCS and Houston's most dynamic player from that team, Carlos Beltran, had signed with the New York Mets during the offseason. But games are won on the field, not on paper, and the Astros managed to win when it counted most, dispatching St. Louis four-games-to-two. Roy Oswalt, who started the clinching game and notched his second win of the series, was named the LCS MVP. The Astros, finally, were on their way to the first World Series in franchise history.

"I'm not selfish or greedy," Houston's veteran second baseman Craig Biggio said, speaking for himself and his 15-year teammate, Jeff Bagwell. "I just wanted to go one time."

The Series opened at Chicago's U.S. Cellular Field, where Journey's *'Don't Stop Believin'* had become the team's theme song, and Jermaine Dye delighted the hometown fans by drilling an opposite-field dinger off of Roger Clemens. Three innings later, Joe Crede rocked reliever Wally Rodriguez with a home run to left-center that broke a 3-3 tie and provided the winning run in the Sox' 5-3 victory. Crede also made two run-saving defensive plays, robbing Ensberg with a runner on third in the sixth and turning the same trick again an inning later when he took a hit away from Biggio with Bagwell on third.

"It doesn't mean anything if we don't win three more," said ChiSox catcher A.J. Pierzynski. "The Astros are really good, so it's going to be tough."

Chicago got an idea of just how tough it would be during their rollercoaster ride in Game 2, a game that went through two ties and four lead changes. Konerko looked as if he had provided the final twist when his seventh-inning grand slam catapulted the Sox to a 6-4 lead. Bobby Jenks couldn't throw the switch against Houston, however, and the Astros came roaring back to tie the belly-tightening game in the top of the ninth on a two-out, pinch-hit single by Jose Vizcaino. The Sox finally brought the ride to an unlikely end in the bottom of the inning when

Mark Buehrle became the first pitcher in World Series history to start and to earn a save in consecutive games.

"Everybody wanted to go out there and win together, said Jermaine Dye. "Everybody was pulling on the same rope."

JERMAINE DYE
2005 WORLD SERIES MVP

PAUL KONERKO

Scott Podsednik, who hadn't hit a single home run during the regular season, drilled a walk-off dinger off of Brad Lidge.

"I've never been in a game like this one," said Sox center fielder Aaron Rowand. "Not one. Ever. Everyone thought last night was exciting, but I hope they tuned in tonight."

As thrilling as the first two games had been, they turned out to be just an appetizer for Game 3, however, which was played in Houston's Minute Maid Park. The Sox, who cuffed Oswalt for five runs in the fifth inning, could have made it easy for themselves by giving better fielding support behind Jon Garland, who yielded only two earned runs in his seven innings of work. But Chicago gave away another pair of unearned runs while Garland was on the mound and the Astros added the tying run on a two-out hit in the bottom of the eighth by Jason Lane. The teams stayed deadlocked through five tingling innings until another unlikely Chicago hero, former Astro Geoff Blum, hit a go-ahead big fly in the top of the 14th inning, and the Sox held on to win the longest game in Series history, 7-5.

The Sox completed their quick but exciting four-game sweep with a 1-0 win behind the right arms of starter Freddy Garcia and Jenks, and the eighth-inning, game-winning single by Dye, the Series MVP. "That's what we came here for," said Ken Williams, pointing to the first World Series trophy that the Sox had earned since 1917. "That's what all the hard work was about."

The 2006 World Series showdown was a clash between the Detroit Tigers and the St. Louis Cardinals, a team that hadn't been expected to get into the Fall Classic without buying tickets. That was an ironic turn for the Redbirds, who had won more regular-season games than any other major league team during the previous two seasons. But the 2006 squad wasn't able to make it into the playoffs until the final day of the schedule. Even their manager, Tony La Russa, had often doubted his team's ability to win the race.

The Redbirds' stretch run was keyed by first baseman Albert Pujols, who had clouted 20 game-winning home runs during the season, which accounted for nearly a quarter of the team's victories. Two of those game-changers were cracked in the final week of the season, which helped lift the slumping Cards to their third straight division title. Big Albert's supporting cast included third baseman Scott Rolen, center fielder Jim Edmonds, and shortstop David Eckstein. Chris Carpenter was the ace of the staff and Jason Marquis and Jeff Suppan followed him in the rotation. Rookie Adam Wainright,

meanwhile, had stepped up smartly as the team's closer after Jason Isringhausen suffered a season-ending injury.

The Cardinals opened their postseason drive by knocking out the San Diego Padres, who had won the West division, three-games-to-one. Pujols continued his season-long heroics with a pair of game-winning RBI and Carpenter also delivered on cue by winning both of his starts. In the League Championship Series, the Redbirds were decided underdogs against the New York Mets, who had led the league with 97 victories. But the two teams turned the series into one of the most memorable in LCS history, with the outcome undecided until the final out of game seven.

The home-team Mets took the opener, 2-0, on a two-run home run by Carlos Beltran, who had nearly derailed the Redbirds' pennant ride two years earlier, when he played for the Houston Astros. The Cards countered with a 9-6 win in the second game, rallying to tie the score on Scott Spiezio's two-run triple in the seventh before getting the go-ahead run on So Taguchi's leadoff homer in the ninth. After the clubs also split the next four games, the stage was set for a dramatic finish to a riveting series and the teams didn't disappoint. The first eight innings offered a tense pitching duel and a 1-1 tie, but in the top of the ninth Cards' catcher Yadier Molina, who hit six home runs and posted a .216 average during the regular season, stepped up and hit a two-run bolt over the left field fence. The Mets battled back in the bottom of the inning, however, and with two outs and the bases loaded the series came down to a duel between the rookie reliever, Adam Wainright, and Carlos Beltran. After Wainright got ahead in the count, 0-2, he decided not to waste a pitch but to go right for the jugular, and he threw a called third strike that buckled Beltran's knees, a sharp-breaking, twelve-to-six curveball that froze him like a statue with a bat.

The Cards' return to the World Series two years after the Boston Red Sox had unexpectedly swept them in 2004 presented an opportunity for redemption for the team, most especially for Rolen and Edmonds, who were a combined 1-for-30 with one RBI against the BoSox. The Redbirds' reprise also provided a first-chance for Chris Carpenter, who missed the 2004 Series with an injury.

Detroit had finished one game behind the Minnesota Twins in the American League's Central division but their 95 wins were good enough to get them into the postseason as the league's wild-card team. The Tigers' lineup was studded with a group of run-producing hitters, including shortstop Carlos Guillen, third baseman Brandon Inge,

and corner outfielders Magglio Ordonez and Craig Monroe. Catcher Ivan Rodriguez, who had a World Series ring from his stint with the 2003 Florida Marlins, handled a pitching staff that was led by a contrasting pair of 17-game winners: Kenny Rogers, an artful southpaw veteran, and Justin Verlander, an overpowering rookie right-hander, whose fastballs exploded into Rodriguez's mitt at nearly 100 miles per hour.

In the Division series, Detroit drew the New York Yankees, who had tied the Mets as the winningest team in the majors. But, after dropping the opener at Yankee Stadium, the Tigers surprised the Yankees by winning three straight and advancing to the LCS against the West division champion Oakland Athletics, who had swept the Twins in the other divisional series. And then, in a bit of payback for the Central division, the Tigers swept the A's, with Magglio Ordonez supplying a dramatic end to the series with a two-out, three-run walk-off jack in the finale.

The Tigers appeared to have the advantage in Game 1 of the World Series, both because they were playing at home in Comerica Park and because they had Verlander, the American League Rookie of the Year, going against Redbirds' rookie Anthony Reyes, who had won only six games during the season. But the Cardinals jumped all over Verlander, roughing him up for seven runs in five innings, while Reyes, who was pressed into service only because the team had depleted

The 83 regular-season wins by the Cardinals was the lowest total ever recorded by a World Series winner.

"People said we couldn't win with our record," said Scott Spiezio. "If that were true, though, why play the games?"

DAVID ECKSTEIN
2006 WORLD SERIES MVP

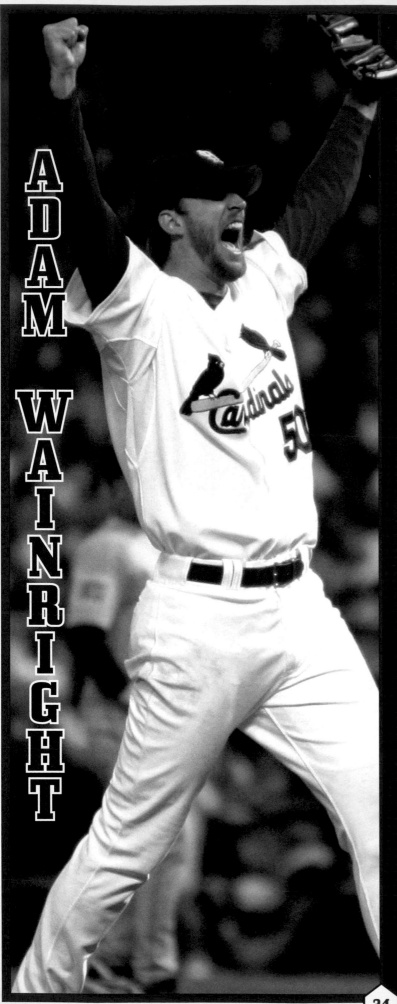

ADAM WAINRIGHT

its staff against the Mets, went eight strong innings in the Redbirds' 7-2 victory. Pujols and Rolen contributed home runs and Edmonds doubled his 2004 World Series hit total and knocked in a run.

The Series produced standout pitching performances over the following two games, as well. Kenny Rogers delivered the first one, checking the Cardinals on two hits over eight innings, as Detroit evened the series with a 3-1 win. Craig Monroe abetted Rogers' sterling effort with a first-inning home run, his second big fly of the Series. The scene shifted to St. Louis for Game 3 and Chris Carpenter was at the top of his game, holding the Tigers to three hits in his eight innings of work, while Edmonds picked up two more RBI in the Redbirds' 5-0 win.

With a two-to-one Series lead and the finish line in sight, the littlest Redbird, their five-foot-seven-inch shortstop, David Eckstein, propelled the team forward in the final two games. In Game 4, Eckstein delivered four hits and a pair of RBI, including the eighth-inning game-winner. And in Game 5, Eckstein, who was named the Series MVP, had two more hits and another pair of RBI, as the Redbirds put the finishing touches on the franchise's 10th World Series title, its first in 24 years.

"No one believed in our club, but we believed in ourselves and went out and took one day at a time," said Eckstein, who became the fourth shortstop to win the MVP Award. "We didn't dwell on the past and we weren't looking towards the future. We stayed just in the moment."

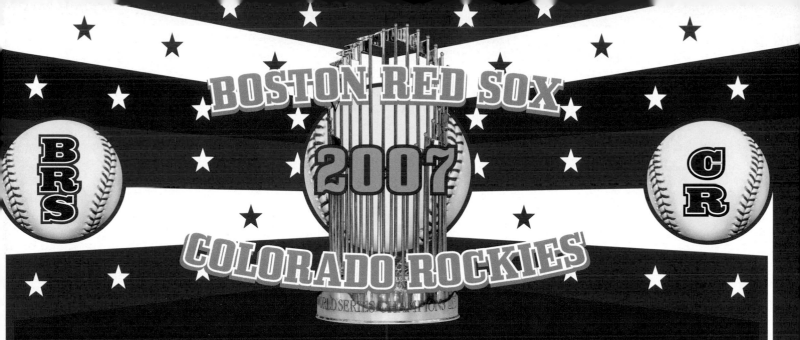

BOSTON RED SOX
2007
COLORADO ROCKIES

The 2007 World Series was a contest between the Boston Red Sox, a team that had led the American League East for the final 166 days of the season, against the Colorado Rockies, a team that had to win a playoff to just qualify as the National League's wild-card team.

The Red Sox were an incredibly well-balanced team, with a slew of dangerous hitters, including third baseman Mike Lowell, who racked up 120 RBI, and designated hitter David Ortiz, who led the team with a .332 average while smoking 35 home runs and driving in 117 runs. The BoSox also received solid contributions from left fielder Manny Ramirez, second baseman Dustin Pedroia, the American League Rookie of the Year, and Kevin Youkilis, who went the entire season without making an error at first base. They also had a staff of gifted pitchers, who had compiled the lowest ERA in the league. 20-game winner Josh Beckett was the ace in a rotation that also included 17 game winner Tim Wakefield, Daisuke Matsuzaka, who won 15 after coming over from Japan, where he had been the country's best pitcher, and Curt Schilling, whose career was finally winding down. The

Red Sox also had a fabulous bullpen, which featured another Japanese player, Hideki Okajima, and the flame-throwing closer Jonathan Papelbon, who posted a microscopic 1.85 ERA and averaged almost 13 strikeouts per nine innings.

This formidable crew swept the Anaheim Angels in the Division series, with Beckett setting the tone with a shutout in the first game and Youkilis supplying the only necessary run with a first-inning solo homer. Ramirez put an exclamation mark on the second game by blasting a three-run walk-off big fly over the *Green Monster* that serves as Fenway Park's left field fence. Schilling, one of the best big-game pitchers of his generation, must have heard the clang of the fire bell before game three, because he tossed seven shutout innings. Ortiz and Ramirez, the big bats in the middle of Boston's lineup went bang-bang back-to-back in the fourth and the Red Sox romped, 9-1.

Boston also snatched the opener of the LCS, 10-3, from Cleveland, the Central division champions, who had eliminated the New York Yankees in the other divisional series. Beckett, the runner-up for the AL Cy Young Award, out-did C.C. Sabathia, who won the award, while Lowell and Ramirez had three RBI each. But Cleveland took the following three games, leaving Boston's World Series prospects thinner than winter sun. Beckett brightened their outlook with another pitching gem, however, holding Cleveland to a single run, while Youkilis drove in three of Boston's seven scores in game five. And Schilling delivered another big-time performance in game six, getting all the runs he would need when right-fielder J. D. Drew dialed up a first-inning grand slam at Fenway. Boston closed out their three-game comeback—evoking memories of their four-game rally against the Yankees in the 2004 LCS—with another blowout win in game seven to advance to their second World Series appearance in four years.

The Rockies, unlike the Red Sox, had stumbled out of the starting gate, at one point dipping nine games under .500, but they turned around their season and, after a finishing kick of 14 wins in their final 15 games, they beat the San Diego Padres in a one-game playoff for the league's final playoff spot.

The biggest stick in the Rockies' lineup belonged to left fielder Matt Holiday, who hit 36 home runs and led the league with 137 RBI and a .340 batting average. Third baseman Garrett Atkins and right fielder Brad Hawpe also topped the century mark in RBI, while their veteran first baseman Todd Helton and shortstop Troy Tulowitski, the league's Rookie of the

Year, both drove in more than 90 runs. Colorado also had a superb defense, which committed only 68 errors and finished first in the league in fielding percentage. The weak link in the Rockies' armor was its pitching staff. Besides Jeff Francis, who went 17-9, only one other starter, Josh Fogg, won even 10 games and the team also lacked a dominant closer.

But the Rockies certainly did have momentum and they continued their season-ending hot streak by sweeping the Philadelphia Phillies in the Division series and the Arizona Diamondbacks in the LCS to capture Colorado's first pennant since the franchise was founded, in 1993. The Rockies, having won 21 of their last 22 games, entered the World Series under a full head of steam, but their magical mystery ride ran into the buzz-saw of reality in the persons of Josh Beckett and the Boston Red Sox.

Beckett came out smoking and never let up, holding the overwhelmed Rockies to one run in seven innings, as the Red Sox romped to a Game 1 win. The lanky right-hander, who had become as automatic as the sun rising in the east, upped his record in the 2007 postseason to 4-0 and lowered his ERA to 1.20.

"He's on top of his game and probably pitching as well as any pitcher I've faced or seen pitch in the postseason," said Rockies' manager Clint Hurdle. "He had command of all his pitches and was just pounding the strike zone. What's he got, 30 innings, a couple of

The Red Sox outscored the Rockies 29-10, the largest scoring differential in a sweep in Series history.

The Red Sox sweep in successive Series appearances was last accomplished by the New York Yankees in 1998-1999.

MIKE LOWELL

2007 WORLD SERIES MVP

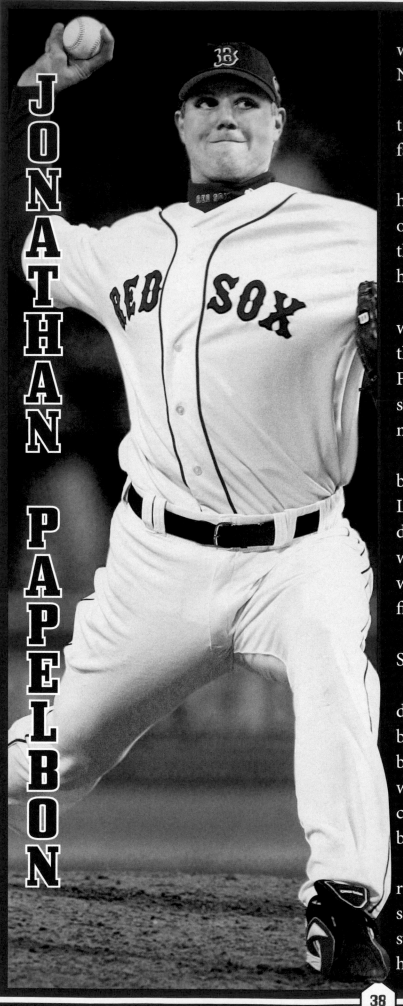

JONATHAN PAPELBON

walks and 35 strikeouts? *Come on.* Those are Nintendo numbers."

For Mike Lowell, his current and former teammate, Beckett's domination had a familiar look to it.

"He's something special," said Lowell. "I saw him do this in 2003 when we were together on the Marlins. I thought that was the best three-week stretch I had seen by a pitcher, and he's doing it again."

The Boston batters had set an early tone when Pedroia cracked a leadoff homer in the bottom of the first and manager Terry Francona's crew pounded Colorado into submission with a seven-run fifth inning that made the final score 13-1.

Runs were scarce in the Game 2 match-up between Schilling and Ubaldo Jiminez, with Lowell breaking a 1-1 tie with a game-winning double in the bottom of the fifth. Schilling, who pitched four-hit ball for 5.1 innings, then watched as Okajima and Papelbon put the finishing touches on what he had started.

"This was the *Pap-ajima Show* tonight," said Schilling. "That was just phenomenal to watch."

The Series shifted to Colorado but the results didn't get any better for the Rockies, as Boston battered them 10-5 in Game 3, with Matsuzaka becoming the first Japanese-born pitcher to win in a World Series game. And then they completed the sweep with a 4-3 win in Game 4 behind left-hander cancer-survivor Jon Lester.

"I started to have this vision of the guys running out of the dugout and tackling me," said Papelbon, who closed out the Series with a strikeout. "You wait your whole life to have that happen. And then all of a sudden you are there."

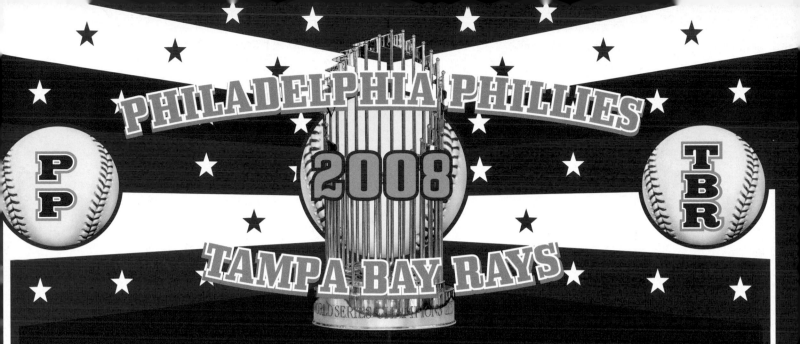

The 2008 World Series was a face-off between the Philadelphia Phillies, a team that was expected to vie for the National League crown, and the Tampa Bay Rays, a team that defied even their own expectations to capture the American League pennant.

"I knew we were going to be good, but never in a million years would I ever have expected this," admitted pitcher Scott Kazmir. "I don't think anyone did, until we got halfway done with the season. After that, we knew—we knew we had something."

The Rays had come into the season with a legacy of losing, the franchise having finished under .500 in each of its 10 previous seasons. But the 2008 team threw off that albatross by winning 97 games and displacing the Boston Red Sox and the New York Yankees, the division's perennial powers, at the top of the AL East.

Kazmir, an 11-game-winner, was part of a rotation that featured five other double-digit winners, including James Shields and Edwin Jackson, who had topped the list with 14 wins each. When their top closer, veteran Troy Percival, suffered a late-season injury, the

remaining members of the bullpen filled the sudden breach. On offense, the Rays didn't have anybody that struck fear into opposing pitchers, other than first baseman Carlos Pena, who racked up 31 homers and 102 RBI, and third baseman Evan Longoria, the AL Rookie of the Year, who drilled 27 dingers and drove in 85 runs, despite missing almost a quarter of the season.

The Rays began their first-ever playoff series with a 6-4 win over the visiting Chicago White Sox at Tropicana Park, as Longoria became only the second player in history to hit home runs in his first two postseason at-bats. After splitting the following two games, the Rays eliminated the ChiSox with a 6-2 win, as center fielder B. J. Upton stroked a pair of big flies and the designated hitter, Cliff Floyd, delivered the go-ahead RBI.

The Rays then hosted the wild-card-winning Red Sox in the opening game of the LCS but Boston turned the tables on their division upstarts with a 2-0 win behind Daisuke Matsuzaka. Tampa Bay bounced back by battering Boston pitching for 10 big flies and 41 runs in the following three games, all of which they won. But the BoSox staved off defeat by taking two-straight and forcing a seventh game showdown. Tampa Bay stepped up to that challenge decisively, as Matt Garza out-dueled Jon Lester, 3-1, and the Rays captured the first pennant in franchise history.

The Phillies were a power-hitting team, starting with first baseman Ryan Howard, who had led the majors with 48 home runs and 146 RBI. Second baseman Chase Utley, Howard's chief comrade-in-arms, had contributed 33 dingers and 104 RBI and substantial numbers had also been produced by corner outfielders Pat Burrell and Jayson Werth, as well as shortstop Jimmy Rollins, who swiped 47 bases. Southpaws Jamie Moyers and Cole Hamels topped the pitching rotation and closer Brad Lidge had saved 41 consecutive games, without blowing a single one.

Philadelphia opened its championship run by beating the Milwaukee Brewers in a tightly-pitched Division series, three-games-to-one. Hamels, who had won the opener of the Milwaukee series, also dominated the Los Angeles Dodgers in the first game of the LCS, as the Phillies won, 3-2, on home runs by Utley and Burrell. Philadelphia closed the series the way it had begun, with Hamels, who was named series MVP, leading the way to a 5-1 win in game four. Rollins drilled the first pitch of the game over the wall and, two innings later, came in to score the go-ahead run on a single by Howard.

Game 1 of the World Series was played at Tropicana Field and closely followed the outcome of the Phillies opening-game win in the LCS, even duplicating the 3-2 score. Utley, again swung the big bat, cracking a two-run jack off of Kazmir, while Hamels, who went seven strong innings, and the bullpen, held the Rays in check. Game 2 was almost a mirror image of the first game, with the Rays striking for a couple of first-inning runs and building their lead up to 4-0 behind the shutout pitching of James Shields. The Phillies closed the gap against rookie southpaw David Price with an eighth-inning pinch-hit solo homer by Eric Bruntlett and an unearned run in the ninth, but the Rays hung on for their first-ever World Series win.

"I was nervous—very nervous," admitted Price, who had entered the game with two out and two men on in the seventh and struck out Ryan Howard. "I don't usually sweat out there but my hat looks as if I went swimming in it."

The scene shifted to Citizens Bank Park for Game 3, where Phillies' fans got to see their first home Series game since 1993. Philadelphia built up an early 4-1 lead, thanks, mainly, to a trio of solo homers: a second inning drive by catcher Carlos Ruiz and back-to-back blasts over the right field wall by Utley and Howard in the sixth. Jamie Moyer, meanwhile, had been cruising along until the Rays nicked him for a pair of runs in the seventh. Then, they tied the game an inning later against Ryan Madson, when center fielder B.J. Upton manufactured a run using his speed on an infield single and swipes

Joe Blanton's home run was the first by a pitcher in a World Series since Ken Holtzman hit one in 1974.

Cole Hamels became the fifth player to win MVP honors in an LCS and World Series in the same season.

COLE HAMEL
2008 WORLD SERIES MVP

RYAN HOWARD

of second and third bases, before gliding home on Ruiz's throwing error. But the slow-running catcher atoned for his error in the bottom of the ninth with a bases-loaded dribbler down the third base line that plated Bruntlett with the winning run.

"This is the kind of World Series you dream of being in," said Howard. "It's nerve-racking, but to come out with a victory like that, it's great."

Howard helped lower the tension level for the Phillies in the following game by blasting a pair of big flies that paved the way to Philadelphia's 10-2 win. Jayson Werth and Joe Blanton, the winning pitcher, also cleared the fences for the Phillies. But the pressure was amplified when rain suspended Game 5 in the middle of the sixth inning, with the score tied 2-2. When play resumed, two nights later, Philadelphia took the lead on an earned run and, after Rocco Baldelli's homer in the seventh re-knotted the game, third baseman Pedro Feliz singled in the go-ahead in the bottom of the inning. Manager Charlie Manuel then put the game in the hands of Brad Lidge and the closer finished it in style by striking out Eric Hinske for his 48th consecutive save and the final out in the Phillies first World Series triumph since 1980 and only its second, overall, in 125 years.

"I never felt better than I do right now," said Lidge. "This is what you dream about."

The 2009 World Series showdown pitted the Philadelphia Phillies, who were going for their second successive title, against the New York Yankees, who were trying to win their first championship since 2000.

The Phillies had cruised to the top of the National League's East division for the third straight season with a power-packed line-up that led the NL in runs scored and home runs. First baseman Ryan Howard set the pace with 45 round-trippers and tied for the league-high 141 RBI. Surrounding Howard in the lineup were second baseman Chase Utley and corner outfielders Jayson Werth and Raul Ibanez, a trio who totaled 101 big flies and 285 RBI. Shortstop Jimmy Rollins, the 2007 MVP, and center fielder Shane Victorino gave them Gold Glove-winners at key positions and speed on the bases. The Phillies had upgraded their starting pitching with a blockbuster mid-season trade for Cliff Lee, the 2008 AL Cy Young Award-winner, and by the signing of three-time Cy Young Award-winner Pedro Martinez. Lee and Martinez joined a quartet of pitchers who each had won 10 or more games, including Joe Blanton, Jamie Moyers,

rookie J.A. Harp, and Cole Hamels. The bullpen, however, had become a big question mark because Brad Lidge, after going through 2008 with 48 consecutive saves, had blown 11 in 2009, the most in either league.

The Phillies began their title trek by beating the Colorado Rockies in the Division series, three-games-to-one. Cliff Lee was in top form in the opener, holding the hard-hitting Rockies to one run in a complete game victory, the first complete game by a Philadelphia pitcher in the postseason since Curt Schilling did it in Game 5 of the 1993 World Series. The Phillies closed out the series with a pair of ninth-inning wins in Colorado, as Howard delivered the game-clinching RBI in the first game and then scored the winning run in the second, after he had doubled in the tying runs.

Philadelphia then steamrolled Los Angeles in the LCS, taking four-of-five, as Howard feasted on Dodgers' pitching and the Phillies won their second consecutive pennant. Howard, who was named the series MVP, drove in eight runs and extended his RBI streak to eight straight postseason games,

ALEX RODRIGUEZ

tying a record set in 1932 by former Yankees' great Lou Gehrig.

"Right now, I'm going to celebrate, enjoy myself a little bit," said Ryan. "To get to this point, to have the opportunity to try to win the World Series two years in a row, that's even more special."

The Yankees, in many ways, were a replica of the Phillies, with a power-generating lineup that had topped the AL in most batting categories, including home runs, with a franchise-record 244. The biggest thumpers were the corner infielders, first baseman Mark Teixeira—who, in his first season with the Yankees, delivered a league-high 122 RBI and tied for the home run title with 39 dingers—and third baseman Alex Rodriguez, who collected 30 homers and 100 RBI for the 12th consecutive year, despite missing nearly a quarter of the schedule with an injury. But the entire line-up was filled with run producers, including designated hitter Hideki Matsui, corner outfielders Johnny Damon and Nick Swisher, second baseman Robinson Cano, and catcher Jorge Posada. The shortstop and team captain, Derek Jeter, posted the league's third-highest batting average, while Cano finished sixth.

The Yankees had signed the league's 2007 Cy Young Award-winner C. C. Sabathia to be the ace of their staff and, as if on cue, he delivered 19 victories. The seemingly ageless Andy Pettitte, with 14 wins, and A.J. Burnett, with 13, followed Sabathia in the rotation. The bullpen was also well-stocked and in a game-saving situation manager Joe Girardi had the luxury of ringing for Mariano Rivera, by acclamation the most dominant and consistent closer of all time.

The Yankees swept three straight from the Minnesota Twins in the Division series, although they had to stage late innings rallies in the concluding two games to get the deed done. Alex Rodriguez, who had been maligned for his failure to deliver in some earlier postseason appearances with the Yankees, hit a pair of game-tying dingers and was the batting star of the series.

The Bronx Bombers then went on to beat the Los Angeles Angels in the LCS, four-games-to-two. Sabathia laid the foundation with a first-game gem at the new Yankee Stadium, and A-Rod hit an 11th-inning big fly over the right field wall that tied the second game, providing the opportunity for the Yankees to pull out the win in the 13th. Rodriguez, in fact, continued his hitting rampage throughout the series, racking up three dingers and six RBI. The Yankees dropped two out of three on the West coast but their 10-1 win in the middle game—behind Sabathia, who was named the LCS MVP—gave them the opportunity to come home and close out the Angels. Which is exactly what they did in the following game, with Andy Pettitte pitching the Yankees to their 40th pennant.

"This is what we play for, this is what we set out for in Spring Training," said Pettitte, who became baseball's all-time leader with his 16th postseason win and also set a record with his fifth career victory to clinch a

postseason series. "To be able to get there and to accomplish that, it's awesome."

Game 1 of the World Series was a match-up of former teammates, Sabathia and Lee, and while Sabathia was good, Lee was even better. The Yankees' southpaw held visiting Philadelphia to only two runs in his seven quality innings, but Lee limited the Yanks to only one unearned run in his complete game win. Chase Utley provided all the necessary runs with a pair of home runs and set a Major League record by reaching base in his 26th consecutive postseason game.

The Yankees evened the Series with a 3-1 win behind superlative starting pitching from A.J. Burnett, who out-dueled Pedro Martinez. Mark Teixeira, playing in his first World Series, tied the game by driving a ball over the right-center field fence in the fourth and Hideki Matsui provided the game-winner with a homer into the right field stands two innings later.

"His home run was huge," said Girardi, who rang for Rivera to get the final six outs. "It's the first lead we've had in this series."

The scene then shifted to Philadelphia for the next three games, where the offense took over center stage. The Phillies jumped on Pettitte for three runs in the second inning of Game 3, with Jayson Werth sparking the outburst with a leadoff home run. A-Rod started the Yankees' comeback and made his first-ever World Series hit a memorable one by lining

The six RBI by Hideki Matsui tied the record that was set by former Yankee Bobby Richardson in 1960.

The World Series triumph was the fifth for Derek Jeter, Jorge Posada, Andy Pettitte, and Mariano Rivera.

ANDY PETTITTE

a two-run homer off of Cole Hamels over the right-field wall—although it took the first video replay in World Series history before it became official. Nick Swisher and Matsui also homered, helping the Yankees to offset a second big fly by Jason Werth and one by Carlos Ruiz and to pull out an 8-5 win. Game 4, in large part, turned on the disparity between the teams' closers, as the game went into the ninth inning knotted at 4-4. Brad Lidge, who had been the Achilles heel of the Phillies' staff, retired the first two batters he faced but couldn't close the door until the Yankees had pushed three runs through it. A-Rod drove in the first run with a double to left and Jorge Posada followed with a two-run RBI single. In the bottom of the ninth, Mariano did what he's done so often, pitched a perfect inning and saved a Yankees' win. The Phillies staved off elimination with an 8-6 win in Game 5, thanks mostly to Utley who got the Phillies going with a three-run homer in the bottom of the first and later hit a solo dinger that proved to be the winning run. His five home runs in a Series tied a record that had been set by former Yankee Reggie Jackson in 1977.

"At some point, maybe I'll look back and see what kind of special moment it is," said Utley. "But right now, our goal is to win two more games."

But the Phillies never reached that goal because Hideki Matsui, who was named the Series MVP, racked up six RBI in Game 6 in support of Pettitte's 18th postseason win, while Rivera recorded his 39th postseason save to put the finishing touch on the Yankees 27th title.

HIDEKI MATSUI
2009 WORLD SERIES MVP

POSTSEASON TRACKER

AMERICAN LEAGUE DIVISION SERIES

	Teams	Score		Teams	Score
G1			G1		
G2			G2		
G3			G3		
G4			G4		
G5			G5		

AMERICAN LEAGUE CHAMPIONSHIP SERIES

	Teams	Score
G1		
G2		
G3		
G4		
G5		
G6		
G7		

NATIONAL LEAGUE DIVISION SERIES

	Teams	Score		Teams	Score
G1			G1		
G2			G2		
G3			G3		
G4			G4		
G5			G5		

NATIONAL LEAGUE CHAMPIONSHIP SERIES

	Teams	Score
G1		
G2		
G3		
G4		
G5		
G6		
G7		

WORLD SERIES

	Teams	Score
G1		
G2		
G3		
G4		
G5		
G6		
G7		

World Series Winner _____